# MAGNETS

by Meg Gaertner

**Cody Koala**

An Imprint of Pop!

popbooksonline.com

abdobooks.com
Published by Pop!, a division of ABDO, PO Box 398166, Minneapolis, Minnesota 55439. Copyright © 2020 by POP, LLC. International copyrights reserved in all countries. No part of this book may be reproduced in any form without written permission from the publisher. Pop!™ is a trademark and logo of POP, LLC.

Printed in the United States of America, North Mankato, Minnesota

052019
092019

**THIS BOOK CONTAINS RECYCLED MATERIALS**

Cover Photo: iStockphoto
Interior Photos: iStockphoto, 1, 11 (top), 11 (bottom left), 11 (bottom right), 12, 19, 21; ELC/Alamy, 5; charistoone-stock/Alamy, 6–7; Jose Luis Pelaez Inc/DigitalVision/Getty Images, 9; Shutterstock Images, 15, 17

Editor: Connor Stratton
Series Designer: Sarah Taplin

Library of Congress Control Number: 2018964776
**Publisher's Cataloging-in-Publication Data**
Names: Gaertner, Meg, author.
Title: Magnets / by Meg Gaertner.
Description: Minneapolis, Minnesota : Pop!, 2020 | Series: Science all around | Includes online resources and index.
Identifiers: ISBN 9781532163586 (lib. bdg.) | ISBN 9781532165023 (ebook)
Subjects: LCSH: Magnets--Juvenile literature. | Magnetism--Juvenile literature. | Science--Juvenile literature.
Classification: DDC 538.4--dc23

## Hello! My name is
# Cody Koala

Pop open this book and you'll find QR codes like this one, loaded with information, so you can learn even more!

Scan this code* and others like it while you read, or visit the website below to make this book pop.

**popbooksonline.com/magnets**

*Scanning QR codes requires a web-enabled smart device with a QR code reader app and a camera.

# Table of Contents

# Chapter 1

# What Is a Magnet?

A boy holds a magnet. He brings **metal** paper clips close to the magnet. Then, he lets the paper clips go. The paper clips shoot toward the magnet. They stick!

Watch a video here!

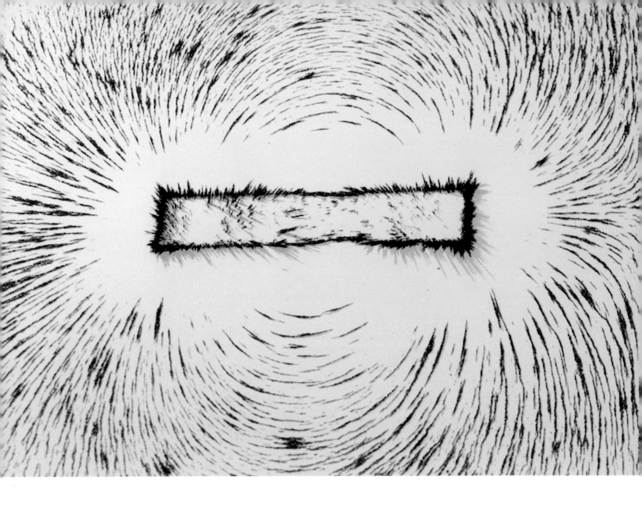

A magnet is anything that
makes a **magnetic field**.
People cannot see the field.

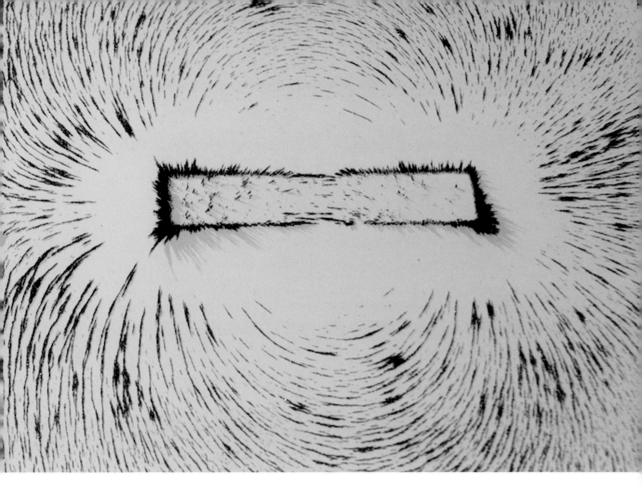

But it surrounds the magnet.

A **force** affects certain

objects in the magnetic field.

This force is called **magnetism**. Magnetism makes some objects move toward one another. It makes other objects move away from one another.

# Chapter 2

# Attraction

Magnets **attract** many **metal** objects. Magnets mostly do not attract nonmetal objects. Some magnets attract objects more strongly than others.

Learn more here!

Some metals can be turned into magnets. People put the metal near a strong **magnetic field**. The metal becomes a magnet for a short time.

# Chapter 3

# Two Poles

Magnets have two ends.
These ends are called the
north and south **poles**.
The **force** of **magnetism** is
strongest at
these poles.

> Earth is a giant magnet. It has a north pole and a south pole.

Learn more here!

North poles **repel** other north poles. South poles repel other south poles. But north and south poles **attract** each other.

## Opposite Poles Attract

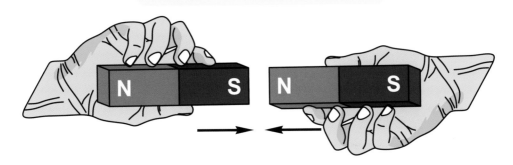

## Like Poles Repel

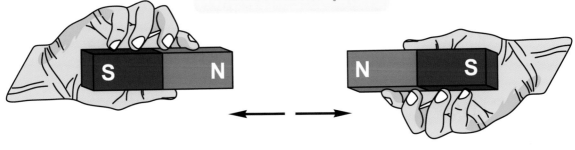

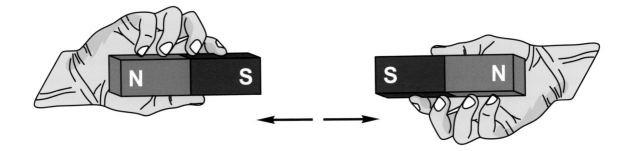

# Chapter 4

# Using Magnets

Compasses use magnets to show direction. Compasses have needles. These needles are tiny magnets. One end swings to point north.

People made early compasses by floating a needle in a bowl of water.

compass needle

Complete an activity here!

Magnets are everywhere. They are inside computers and cars. They keep refrigerators shut tightly. Magnets in MRI machines help doctors see why some people are sick or injured.

People have been using magnets for thousands of years.

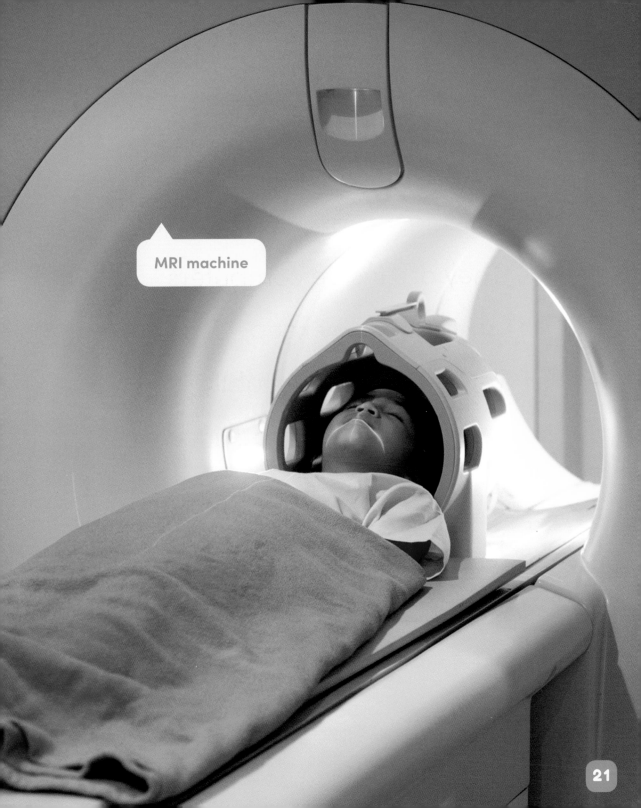

# Making Connections

## Text-to-Self

Have you ever used a magnet? What did it stick to?

## Text-to-Text

Magnetism is a force. Have you read other books about forces? What did you learn?

## Text-to-World

People use magnets to do many things. Where do you see magnets in your life?

# Glossary

**attract** – to make something move closer.

**force** – something that changes the motion of an object.

**magnetic field** – the area surrounding a magnet. Magnetism affects objects in this area.

**magnetism** – a force that causes objects to be attracted to or repelled by one another.

**metal** – a shiny, hard material.

**pole** – one of the two opposite ends of a magnet where the magnetic forces are the strongest.

**repel** – to make something move away.

# Index

## Online Resources

# popbooksonline.com

Thanks for reading this Cody Koala book!

Scan this code* and others like it in this book, or visit the website below to make this book pop!

**popbooksonline.com/magnets**

*Scanning QR codes requires a web-enabled smart device with a QR code reader app and a camera.